REALLY EASY GUITAR

POP SONGS FOR KIDS

22 SONGS WITH CHORDS, LYRICS & BASIC TAB

T0071383

ISBN 978-1-5400-4077-0

For all works contained herein:
Unauthorized copying, arranging, adapting, recording, Internet posting, public performance,
or other distribution of the music in this publication is an infringement of copyright.
Infringers are liable under the law.

Visit Hal Leonard Online at
www.halleonard.com

Contact us:
Hal Leonard
7777 West Bluemound Road
Milwaukee, WI 53213
Email: info@halleonard.com

In Europe, contact:
Hal Leonard Europe Limited
42 Wigmore Street
Marylebone, London, W1U 2RN
Email: info@halleonardeurope.com

In Australia, contact:
Hal Leonard Australia Pty. Ltd.
4 Lentara Court
Cheltenham, Victoria, 3192 Australia
Email: info@halleonard.com.au

GUITAR NOTATION LEGEND

Chord Diagrams

CHORD DIAGRAMS graphically represent the guitar fretboard to show correct chord fingerings.

- The letter above the diagram tells the name of the chord.
- The top, bold horizontal line represents the nut of the guitar. Each thin horizontal line represents a fret. Each vertical line represents a string; the low E string is on the far left and the high E string is on the far right.
- A dot shows where to put your fret-hand finger and the number at the bottom of the diagram tells which finger to use.
- The "O" above the string means play it open, while an "X" means don't play the string.

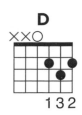

Tablature

TABLATURE graphically represents the guitar fingerboard. Each horizontal line represents a string, and each number represents a fret.

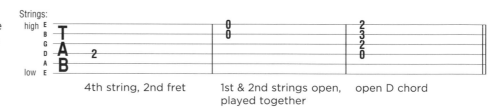

4th string, 2nd fret   1st & 2nd strings open, played together   open D chord

Definitions for Special Guitar Notation

HAMMER-ON: Strike the first (lower) note with one finger, then sound the higher note (on the same string) with another finger by fretting it without picking.

PULL-OFF: Place both fingers on the notes to be sounded. Strike the first note and without picking, pull the finger off to sound the second (lower) note.

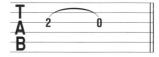

LEGATO SLIDE: Strike the first note and then slide the same fret-hand finger up or down to the second note. The second note is not struck.

SHIFT SLIDE: Same as legato slide, except the second note is struck.

Additional Musical Definitions

N.C.   • No chord. Instrument is silent.

• Repeat measures between signs.

Bad Day

Words and Music by Daniel Powter

(Capo 1st Fret)

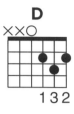
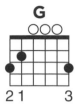
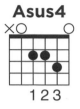
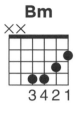
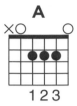

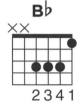
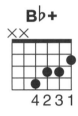

INTRO

Moderately

| D | | G | | Asus4 | | |

VERSE 1

D   G   Asus4   D   G   Asus4

Where is the moment we needed the most?   You kick up the leaves, and the magic is lost.

PRE-CHORUS 1

Bm   A   G   D   Em

They tell me your blue skies fade to grey. They tell me your passion's gone away,

A

and I don't need no carryin' on.

VERSE 2

D   G   Asus4   D   G   Asus4

You stand in the line just to hit a new low.   You're fakin' a smile with the coffee to go.

PRE-CHORUS 2

Bm   A   G   D   Em

They tell me your life's been way off line. You've fallen to pieces every time,

A N.C.

and I don't need no carryin' on because

CHORUS 1

D   G   Em   A

You had a bad day. You're takin' one down. You sing a sad song just to turn it around.

D   G   Em   A

You say you don't know. You tell me don't lie. You work at a smile, and you go for a ride.

Bm   D   G   D

You had a bad day. The camera don't lie. You're comin' back down, and you really don't mind.

Em   A

You had a bad day.   You had a bad

Copyright © 2005 Song 6 Music
All Rights Administered by BMG Rights Management (US) LLC
All Rights Reserved Used by Permission

INTERLUDE

```
D                          G                      Asus4
‖: day.              |                   |                      |          :‖
```

PRE-CHORUS 3

```
Bm              A        G              D              Em
       Well, you need a blue sky holiday. The point is they laugh at what you say,

                        Asus4        A
and I don't need no carryin' on.
```

CHORUS 2

```
              D          G              Em              A
You had a bad day. You're takin' one down. You sing a sad song just to turn it around.

              D          G              Em              A
You say you don't know. You tell me don't lie. You work at a smile, and you go for a ride.

              Bm         D              G              D
You had a bad day. The camera don't lie. You're comin' back down, and you really don't mind.

              Em
You had a bad day, ooh, on a holiday.
```

BRIDGE

```
F                              B♭
Sometimes the system goes on the blink and the whole thing, it turns out wrong.

    F                              B♭
You might not make it back, and you know that you could be, well, that strong, and I'm not

D          A
wrong, yeah, yeah.
```

VERSE 3

```
D          G              Asus4
    So where is the passion when you need it the most? Oh, you and

D          G              A
I. You kick up the leaves, and the magic is lost 'cause
```

CHORUS 3

```
              D          G              Em              A
You had a bad day. You're takin' one down. You sing a sad song just to turn it around.

              D          G              Em              A
You say you don't know. You tell me don't lie. You work at a smile, and you go for a ride.

              Bm         B♭+            D              E7
You had a bad day. You've seen what you like. And how does it feel one more time?

              G    Asus4           D    G    Em    A
You had a bad day.           You had a bad day.
```

OUTRO   *REPEAT AND FADE*

```
‖: D              | G              | Em              | A              :‖
```

Beat It

Words and Music by Michael Jackson

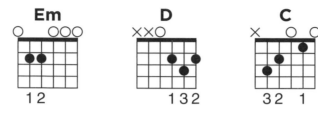

INTRO

Moderately fast

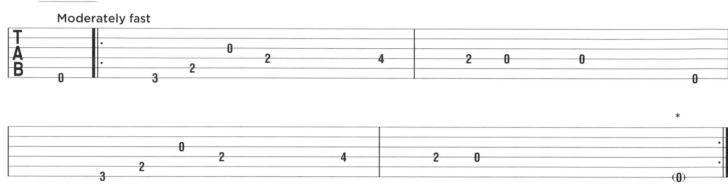

*Omit
2nd time

VERSE 1

Em **D** **Em**
They told him, "Don't you ever come around here. Don't wanna see your face. You better

D **C** **D** **Em** **D**
disappear." The fire's in their eyes, and their words are really clear. So beat it, just beat it.

Em **D** **Em** **D**
You better run; you better do what you can. Don't wanna see no blood. Don't be a macho man.

C **D** **Em** **D**
You wanna be tough; better do what you can. So beat it, but you wanna be bad.

CHORUS

w/ Intro Riff
Just beat it, beat it. No one wants to be defeated.

Showin' how funky, strong is your fight. It doesn't matter who's wrong or right.

INTERLUDE

w/ Intro Riff
Just beat it, just beat it, just beat it, just beat it.

Copyright © 1982 Mijac Music
All Rights Administered by Sony/ATV Music Publishing LLC, 424 Church Street, Suite 1200, Nashville, TN 37219
International Copyright Secured   All Rights Reserved

VERSE 2

Em   D   Em   D

They're out to get you; better leave while you can. Don't wanna be a boy; you wanna be a man.

C   D   Em   D

You wanna stay alive; better do what you can. So beat it, just beat it.

Em   D   Em

You have to show them that you're really not scared. You're playing with your life; this ain't no

D   C   D

truth or dare. They'll kick you, then they beat you, then they'll tell you it's fair.

Em   D

So beat it, but you wanna be bad.

REPEAT CHORUS (2 TIMES)

BRIDGE

Play 4 times

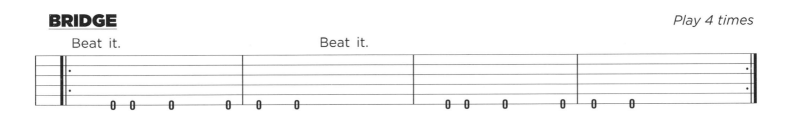

Beat it.   Beat it.

REPEAT CHORUS (REPEAT AND FADE)

Beautiful Day

Words by Bono
Music by U2

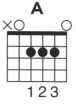 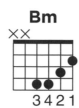 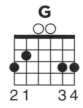  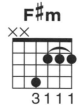 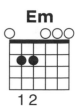

INTRO

Moderately

‖: A   Bm   D | G | D   A | :‖

VERSE 1

A   Bm   D   G   D   A
The heart is a bloom,   shoots up through the stony ground.

Bm   D   G   D   A
But there's no room,   no space to rent in this town.

Bm   D   G   D   A
You're out of luck   and the reason that you had to care.

Bm   D   G   D   A
The traffic is stuck,   and you're not moving anywhere.

Bm   D   G   D   A
You thought you'd found a friend   to take you out of this place,

Bm   D   G   D   A
someone you could lend a hand   in return for grace.

CHORUS 1

A   Bm   D   G   D   A
It's a beautiful day,   sky falls. You feel like

Bm   D   G   D   A
it's a beautiful day,   don't let it get away.

VERSE 2

A   Bm   D   G   D   A
You're on the road,   but you've got no destination.

Bm   D   G   D   A
You're in the mud   in the maze of her imagination.

Bm   D   G   D   A
You love this town   even if that doesn't ring true.

Bm   D   G   D   A
You've been all over,   and it's been all over you.

Copyright © 2000 UNIVERSAL - POLYGRAM INTERNATIONAL MUSIC PUBLISHING B.V.
All Rights in the United States and Canada Controlled and Administered by UNIVERSAL - POLYGRAM INTERNATIONAL PUBLISHING, INC.
All Rights Reserved   Used by Permission

CHORUS 2

            A   Bm   D   G   D   A
It's a beautiful day,   don't let it get away.

                  Bm   D   G   D   A
It's a beautiful day,   ooh, ooh, ooh.

F#m   G   D   A   F#m   G   D   A
Touch me,   take me to that other place. Teach me,   I know I'm not a hopeless case.

REPEAT INTRO (1 TIME)

BRIDGE

Em   D
See the world in green and blue.   See China right in front of you.

Em   G   D
See the canyons broken by cloud.   See the tuna fleets clearing the sea out.

Em   G   D
See the Bedouin fires at night.   See the oil fields at first light, and

Em   G   D   A
see the bird with a leaf in her mouth.   After the flood, all the colors came out.

REPEAT INTRO (1 TIME)

CHORUS 3

             A   Bm   D   G   D   A
It was a beautiful day,   don't let it get away.

                  Bm   D   G   D   A
Beautiful day.

F#m   G   D   A   F#m   G   D   A
Touch me,   take me to that other place. Reach me,   I know I'm not a hopeless case.

             Bm   D   G   D   A
What you don't have, you don't need it now. What you don't know, you can feel it somehow.

             Bm   D   G   D   A
What you don't have, you don't need it now, don't need it now.   Was a beautiful

‖:   Bm   D   G   D   A   :‖
day. | | | | |

OUTRO

A Bm D | G | D   A | | Bm D | G   ‖

Brave

Words and Music by Sara Bareilles and Jack Antonoff

(Capo 3rd Fret)

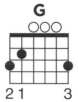 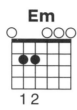 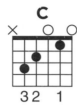 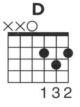 

VERSE 1

Moderately slow

G
You can be amazin', you can turn a phrase into a weapon or a drug.

Em
You can be the outcast or be the backlash of somebody's lack of love,

C   **D**
or you can start speaking up.

G
Nothin's gonna hurt you the way that words do when they settle 'neath your skin,

Em
kept on the inside and no sunlight. Sometimes a shadow

C   **D**   **N.C.**
wins.   But I wonder what would happen if you

CHORUS 1

G   **Em**   **C**   **D**
say what you wanna say,   and let the words fall out honestly.   I wanna see you be brave

G   **Em**   **C**   **D**
with what you wanna say,   and let the words fall out honestly.   I wanna see you be brave.

G   **C**   **Em**   **D**
I just wanna see you. I just wanna see you. I just wanna see you.   I wanna see you be brave.

G   **C**   **Em**   **D**
I just wanna see you. I just wanna see you. I just wanna see you.   I wanna see you be brave.

VERSE 2

G
Everybody's been there, everybody's been stared down by the enemy.

Em
Fallen for the fear and done some disappearin', bow down to the mighty.

C   **D**
Don't run.   Stop holdin' your tongue.

G
Maybe there's a way out of the cage where you live.

Copyright © 2013 Sony/ATV Music Publishing LLC, Tiny Bear Music and Ducky Donath Music
All Rights Administered by Sony/ATV Music Publishing LLC, 424 Church Street, Suite 1200, Nashville, TN 37219
International Copyright Secured   All Rights Reserved

Em
    Maybe one of these days you can let the light

C   **D**   **N.C.**
in, and show me   how big your brave is.

CHORUS 2

G   **Em**   **C**   **D**
Say what you wanna say,   and let the words fall out honestly.   I wanna see you be brave

G   **Em**   **C**   **D**
with what you wanna say,   and let the words fall out honestly.   I wanna see you be brave.

BRIDGE

Em   **G**   **C**   **G**   **C**
And since your history of silence won't do you any good, did you think it would?

Em   **G**   **Dsus4**   **D**
Let your words be anything but empty.   Why don't you tell them the truth?

CHORUS 3

N.C.
say what you wanna say, and let the words fall out honestly. I wanna see you be brave

G   **Em**   **C**   **D**
with what you wanna say,   and let the words fall out honestly.   I wanna see you be brave.

G   **C**   **Em**   **D**
I just wanna see you. I just wanna see you. I just wanna see you.   I wanna see you be brave.

G   **C**   **Em**   **D**
I just wanna see you. I just wanna see you. I just wanna see you.   See you be brave.

OUTRO

G   **C**   **Em**   **D**
I just wanna see you. I just wanna see you. I just wanna see you.

G   **C**   **Em**   **D**
I just wanna see you. I just wanna see you. I just wanna see you.

Can't Stop the Feeling

from TROLLS

Words and Music by Justin Timberlake, Max Martin and Shellback

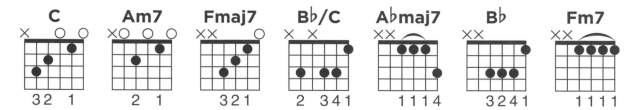

INTRO

Moderately

| C | | Am7 | | Fmaj7 | | Am7 | |

VERSE 1

      C   Am7   Fmaj7   Am7

I got this feeling inside my bones. It goes electric, wavy when I turn it on.

           C   Am7   Fmaj7   Am7

All through my city, all through my home. We're flyin' up, no ceilin' when we in our zone.

VERSE 2

      C   Am7

I got that sunshine in my pocket, got that good soul in my feet.

      Fmaj7   Am7

I feel that hot blood in my body when it drops, ooh.

      C   Am7   Fmaj7   Am7

I can't take my eyes up off it, movin' so phenomenally. Room on lock the way we rock it, so don't stop.

PRE-CHORUS

      Bb/C   C   Bb/C   C

And under the lights when everything goes, nowhere to hide when I'm gettin' you close.

      Abmaj7   Bb   Fm7   Abmaj7

When we move, well you already know. So just imagine, just imagine, just imagine.

CHORUS 1

C   Am7

Nothin' I can see but you when you dance, dance, dance.

      Fmaj7   Am7

I feel a good, good creepin' up on you, so just dance, dance, dance. Come on!

C   Am7

All those things I shouldn't do, but you dance, dance, dance.

      Fmaj7   Am7

And ain't nobody leavin' soon, so keep dancin'.

Copyright © 2016 by Universal Music - Z Tunes LLC, Tennman Tunes, DWA Songs and MXM
All Rights for Tennman Tunes Administered by Universal Music - Z Tunes LLC
All Rights for DWA Songs Administered by Almo Music Corp.
All Rights for MXM Administered Worldwide by Kobalt Songs Music Publishing
International Copyright Secured   All Rights Reserved

CHORUS 2

               C   Am7
I can't stop the feelin', so just dance, dance, dance.

               Fmaj7   Am7
I can't stop the feelin', so just dance, dance, dance. Come on!

VERSE 3

C   Am7   Fmaj7   Am7
    Ooh, it's somethin' magical. It's in the air; it's in my blood; it's rushin' on.

               C   Am7   Fmaj7   Am7
I don't need no reason, don't need control. I fly so high, no ceilin' when I'm in my zone. 'Cause

REPEAT VERSE 2

REPEAT PRE-CHORUS

REPEAT CHORUS 1

CHORUS 3

               C   Am7   Fmaj7   Am7
I can't stop the feelin', so just dance, dance, dance. I can't stop the feelin', so just dance, dance, dance.

               C   Am7   Fmaj7   Am7
I can't stop the feelin', so just dance, dance, dance. I can't stop the feelin', so keep dancin'.

BRIDGE

C   Am7   Fmaj7   Am7
                          | | | I can't stop the, |

C   Am7   Fmaj7
                              | I can't stop the, | |

Am7
                            I can't stop the, | N.C.   I can't stop the, I can't stop the... ||

REPEAT CHORUS 1

CHORUS 4

               C   Am7   Fmaj7   Am7
I can't stop the feelin'. Got this feelin' in my body. I can't stop the feelin'. Got this feelin' in my body.

               C   Am7
I can't stop the feelin'. Wanna see you move your body.

             Fmaj7   Am7
I can't stop the feelin'. Got this feelin' in my body. Come on.

OUTRO

    N.C.
Got this feelin' in my body. I can't stop the feelin'. Got this feelin' in my body. Come on.

Crazy Little Thing Called Love

Words and Music by Freddie Mercury

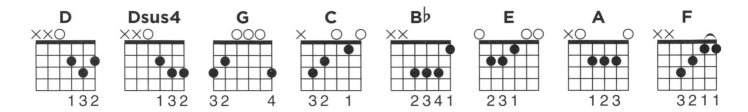

INTRO

Moderately fast

‖: D   Dsus4   D | D   Dsus4   D   :‖

VERSE 1

            D   G   C   G   D

This thing   called love,   I just   can't handle it.   This thing   called love,   I must

G   C   G   D   Bb   C   D   N.C.

get 'round to it. I ain't ready. Crazy little thing called love.

VERSE 2

            D   G   C   G   D

A, this thing   called love,   it cries   in a cradle all night.   It swings,   it jives,

G   C   G   D   Bb   C   D   N.C.

shakes all over like a jellyfish. I kinda like it. Crazy little thing called love.

BRIDGE

               G   C   G   Bb

There goes my baby, she knows how to rock and roll. She drives me crazy.

               E   A   F   N.C.

She gives me hot and cold fever. She leaves me in a cool, cool sweat.

VERSE 3

            D   G   C   G   D

I've gotta be cool,   relax,   get hip,   get on my tracks. Take a backseat,   hitch-hike,

G   C   G   D   Bb   C   D   N.C.

and take a long ride on my motorbike until I'm ready. Crazy little thing called love.

Copyright © 1979 Queen Music Ltd.
All Rights Administered by Sony/ATV Music Publishing LLC, 424 Church Street, Suite 1200, Nashville, TN 37219
International Copyright Secured   All Rights Reserved

INTERLUDE

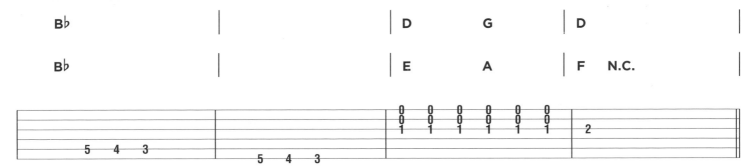

| Bb | | | D | G | D | |
| Bb | | | E | A | F N.C. | |

VERSE 4

N.C.
I've gotta be cool,   relax,   get hip,   get on my tracks. Take a backseat,   hitch-hike,

and take a long ride on my motorbike until I'm ready. Crazy little thing called love.

REPEAT VERSE 1

OUTRO (REPEAT AND FADE)

Bb   C   D   Bb   C   D
Crazy little thing called love. Crazy little thing called love.

Happy

from DESPICABLE ME 2
Words and Music by Pharrell Williams

(Capo 1st Fret)

 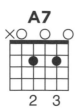 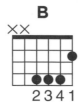 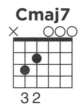 

VERSE 1

E7	N.C.		E7	A7	B	A7
	It might seem crazy what I'm 'bout to say.					

E7	N.C.		E7	A7	B	A7	
	Sunshine, she's here; you can take a break.						I'm a

E7	N.C.		E7	A7	B	A7	
	hot air balloon that could go to space						with the air

E7	N.C.		E7	A7	B	A7
	like I don't care, baby, by the way.					

CHORUS

	Cmaj7	Bm7		E7
Because I'm happy. Clap along if you feel like a room without a roof.				

	Cmaj7	Bm7		E7
Because I'm happy. Clap along if you feel like happiness is the truth.				

	Cmaj7	Bm7		E7
Because I'm happy. Clap along if you know what happiness is to you.				

	Cmaj7	Bm7		E7
Because I'm happy. Clap along if you feel like that's what you wanna do.				

VERSE 2

E7	N.C.		E7	A7	B	A7
	Here come bad news, talkin' this and that.					

E7	N.C.		E7	A7	B	A7
	Well, gimme all you got, and don't hold it back.					

E7	N.C.		E7	A7	B	A7
	Well, I should prob'ly warn you, I'll be just fine.					

E7	N.C.		E7	A7	B	A7
	No offense to you, don't waste your time.			Here's why:		

REPEAT CHORUS

Copyright © 2013 EMI April Music Inc., More Water From Nazareth and Universal Pictures Global Music
All Rights on behalf of EMI April Music Inc. and More Water From Nazareth Administered by Sony/ATV Music Publishing LLC,
424 Church Street, Suite 1200, Nashville, TN 37219
All Rights on behalf of Universal Pictures Global Music Controlled and Administered by Universal Music Works
International Copyright Secured   All Rights Reserved

BRIDGE

N.C.

    Bring me down, can't nothin' bring me down. Your love is too high.

Bring me down, can't nothin' bring me down. I said...

REPEAT BRIDGE

REPEAT CHORUS (2 TIMES)

REPEAT BRIDGE

REPEAT CHORUS (2 TIMES)

Havana

Words and Music by Camila Cabello, Louis Bell, Pharrell Williams, Adam Feeney, Ali Tamposi, Brian Lee, Andrew Wotman, Brittany Hazzard, Jeffery Lamar Williams and Kaan Gunesberk

(Capo 3rd Fret)

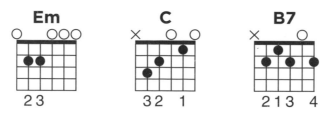

INTRO

Moderately

| Em | C | B7 | | | Em | C | B7 | |

CHORUS 1

Em   C B7   Em   C B7
Havana, ooh, na, na.   Half of my heart is in Havana, ooh, na, na.   He took me back to East

Em   C B7   Em   C   B7 N.C.
Atlanta, na, na, na.   All of my heart is in Havana, there's somethin' 'bout his manners. Havana, ooh, na.

VERSE 1

Em   C   B7 Em   C   B7
He didn't walk up with that, "How you doin'?" He said, "There's a lot of girls I can do with."

Em   C   B7 Em   C   B7
I'm doin' forever in a minute. And Papa says he got malo in him. He got me feelin' like,

Em   C   B7   Em   C   B7
ooh.   I knew it when I met him. I loved him when I left him. Got me feelin' like,

Em   C   B7   Em   C   B7   N.C.
ooh.   And then I had to tell him I had to go.   Oh, na, na, na, na, na.

CHORUS 2

Em   C B7   Em   C B7
Havana, ooh, na, na.   Half of my heart is in Havana, ooh, na, na.   He took me back to East

Em   C B7   Em   C   B7
Atlanta, na, na, na.   All of my heart is in Havana. My heart is in Havana. Havana, ooh, na, na.

Copyright © 2017 Maidmetal Limited, Milamoon Songs, Sony/ATV Music Publishing (UK), EMI April Music Inc., EMI Pop Music Publishing,
More Water From Nazareth, EMI Blackwood Music Inc., EMI Music Publishing Ltd., Nyankingmusic, Sam Fam Beats, Reservoir 416,
Songs of YSL Music Publishing, Songs From The Dong, Andrew Watt Music, People Over Planes, These Are Songs Of Pulse,
300 Rainwater Music, Atlantic Songs and Warner-Tamerlane Publishing Corp.
All Rights on behalf of Maidmetal Limited, Milamoon Songs, Sony/ATV Music Publishing (UK), EMI April Music Inc., EMI Pop Music Publishing,
More Water From Nazareth, EMI Blackwood Music Inc., EMI Music Publishing Ltd., Nyankingmusic and Sam Fam Beats
Administered by Sony/ATV Music Publishing LLC, 424 Church Street, Suite 1200, Nashville, TN 37219
All Rights on behalf of Reservoir 416 and Songs of YSL Music Publishing Administered Worldwide by Reservoir Media Management, Inc.
All Rights on behalf of Songs From The Dong, 300 Rainwater Music and Atlantic Songs Administered by Warner-Tamerlane Publishing Corp.
All Rights on behalf of Andrew Watt Music Administered Worldwide by Songs of Kobalt Music Publishing
All Rights on behalf of People Over Planes Administered by These Are Songs Of Pulse
International Copyright Secured   All Rights Reserved

VERSE 2

N.C.
Jeffery. Just graduated, fresh on campus, mmm. Fresh out East Atlanta with no manners, damn.

Em   C   B7   **Em   C   B7**
Bump on her bumper like a traffic jam.   Hey,   I was quick to pay that girl like Uncle Sam.

N.C. Em   C B7
Back it on me. Shawty cravin' on me. Get to diggin' on me.

Em   C B7
She waited on me. Shawty cakin' on me, got the bacon on me.

Em   C   B7
This is history in the makin' on me.   Point blank, close range that be.

Em   C   B7 N.C.
If it cost a million that's me.   I was gettin' mula, baby.

REPEAT CHORUS 2

BRIDGE

Em   **C**   **B7**
‖:Ooh,   oh,   na,   na, | na.   Take me back, back, back, back. |

Em   **C**   **B7**
Ooh,   na,   na,   oh,   na,   na, | na.   Take me back, back, back. :‖

REPEAT INTRO

INTERLUDE

Em   **C**   **B7**   **Em**   **C**   **B7**
Ooh. | | Ooh.   ‖

REPEAT CHORUS 2

OUTRO   *Play 3 times*

Em   **C**   **B7**
‖:   Oh,   na,   na, | na.   :‖

Em   **C**   **B7** **N.C.**
Oh, na, na, | na.   Ha-van - a, ooh, na, | na.   ‖

Hello

Words and Music by Adele Adkins and Greg Kurstin

(Capo 1st Fret)

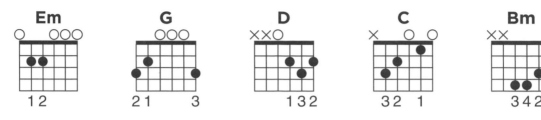

INTRO

Moderately slow

Em	G	D	C	

VERSE 1

Em **G** **D** **C**   **Em** **G** **D** **C**
Hello,   it's me.   I was wondering if after all these years you'd like to meet to go

Em **G** **D** **C**   **Em** **G** **D** **C**
over   everything.   They say that time's supposed to heal you, but I ain't done much healing.

Em **G** **D** **C** **Em** **G** **D** **C**
Hello,   can you hear me?   I'm in California, dreaming about who we used to be when we were

Em **G** **D** **C** **Em** **G** **D** **C**
younger   and free.   I've forgotten how it felt before the world fell at our feet.

PRE-CHORUS 1

Em **D** **Bm** **C** **Em** **D** **C**
There's such a difference   between us and a mil - li - on miles.

CHORUS

Em **C** **G** **D** **Em** **C** **G** **D**
Hello from the other side,   I must have called a thousand times   to tell you

Em **C** **G** **D** **Em** **C** **G** **D**
  I'm sorry for everything that I've done, but when I call,   you never seem to be home.

Em **C** **G** **D** **Em** **C** **G** **D**
Hello from the outside.   At least I can say that I've tried   to tell you

Em **C** **G** **D** **Em** **C** **G** **D**
  I'm sorry for breaking your heart. But it don't matter, it clearly doesn't tear you apart anymore.

REPEAT INTRO

Copyright © 2015 MELTED STONE PUBLISHING LTD., EMI APRIL MUSIC INC. and KURSTIN MUSIC
All Rights for MELTED STONE PUBLISHING LTD. in the U.S. and Canada Administered by
UNIVERSAL - SONGS OF POLYGRAM INTERNATIONAL, INC.
All Rights for EMI APRIL MUSIC INC. and KURSTIN MUSIC Administered by SONY/ATV MUSIC PUBLISHING LLC,
424 Church Street, Suite 1200, Nashville, TN 37219
All Rights Reserved   Used by Permission

VERSE 2

| Em | G | D | C | Em | G | D | C |

Hello, how are you? It's so typical of me to talk about myself; I'm sorry.

| Em | G | D | C | Em | G | D | C |

I hope that you're well. Did you ever make it out of that town where nothing ever happened?

PRE-CHORUS 2

| Em | D | Bm | C | Em | D | C |

It's no secret that the both of us are running out of time. So

REPEAT CHORUS

INTERLUDE

Play 3 times

| Em | C | D | G | Em | C | D | |

‖: Em C | D G | Em C | D ‖
        ooh,   anymore, :   anymore.

REPEAT CHORUS

OUTRO

| Em G | D C | Em | ‖

Home

Words and Music by Greg Holden and Drew Pearson

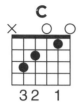
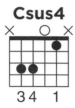

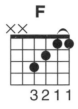
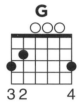

INTRO

Moderately

‖: C | Csus4 | :‖

VERSE 1

C   **Csus4**   **C**   **Csus4**
Hold on   to me as we go.   As we

C   **Csus4**   **C**   **Csus4**
roll down   this unfamiliar road.   And although this

Am   **Csus4**   **C**   **Csus4**
wave   is stringing us along,   just

know   you're   not   a - lone,

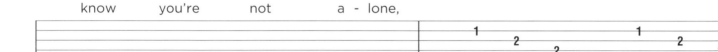

'cause I'm gon - na make this place your

C
home.

VERSE 2

C   **Csus4**   **C**   **Csus4**
Settle down,   it'll all be clear.

C   **Csus4**   **C**   **Csus4**
Don't pay no mind to the demons; they fill you with fear.

Am   **F**   **C**   **G**
Trouble, it might drag you down. You get lost, you can always be found.   Just

Copyright © 2012 FALLEN ART MUSIC, DREWYEAH MUSIC and SONGS OF PULSE RECORDING
All Rights for FALLEN ART MUSIC Administered by WB MUSIC CORP.
All Rights for DREWYEAH MUSIC Administered by SONGS OF PULSE RECORDING
All Rights Reserved   Used by Permission

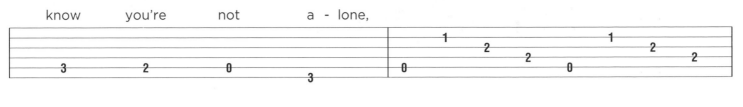

know   you're   not   a - lone,

'cause I'm   gon - na   make   this   place   your

C
home.

CHORUS

| **F** | **C** | **Am** | **G** |
| Ooh, | | ooh, | |

| **F** | **C** | **G** | |
| ooh. | | | |

| **F** | **C** | **Am** | **G** |
| Oh, | | oh, | |

| **F** | **C** | **G** | |
| oh. | | | |

REPEAT VERSE 2

OUTRO

| **F** | **C** | **Am** | **G** |
| Oh, | | oh, | |

| **F** | **C** | **G** | |
| oh. | | | |

| **F** | **C** | **Am** | **G** |
| Oh, | | oh, | |

| **F** | **C** | **G** | |
| oh. | | | |

I Love Rock 'n Roll

Words and Music by Alan Merrill and Jake Hooker

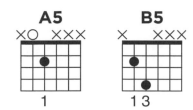

INTRO

Moderately slow

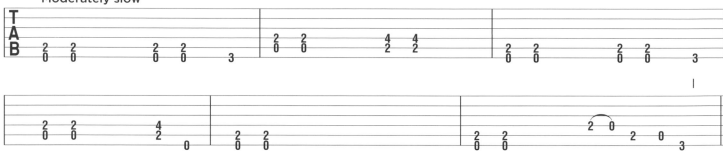

VERSE 1

saw him danc - in' there by the rec-ord ma - chine.   I

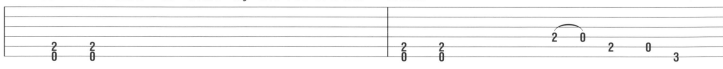

knew he must have been a-bout sev - en - teen.   The

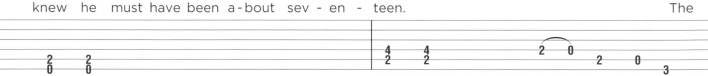

beat was go - in' strong,   play - in' my fav - 'rite

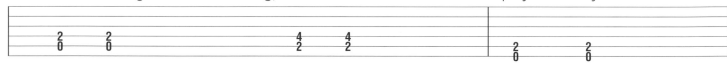

A5   **N.C.**
song. And I could tell it wouldn't be long till he was with me, yeah, me.

                                                   B5
And I could tell it wouldn't be long till he was with me, yeah, me, singin',

CHORUS 1

w/ Intro Riff
I love rock 'n' roll, so put another dime in the jukebox, baby.

I love rock 'n' roll, so come, and take your time, and dance with me.   He

VERSE 2

smiled, so I got up and asked for his name.

Copyright © 1975, 1982 Finchley Music Corp. and RAK Publishing Ltd.
Copyright Renewed
All Rights for the U.S. and Canada Administered by Kobalt Songs Music Publishing
International Copyright Secured   All Rights Reserved

"That don't mat-ter," he said, "'cause it's all the same." I

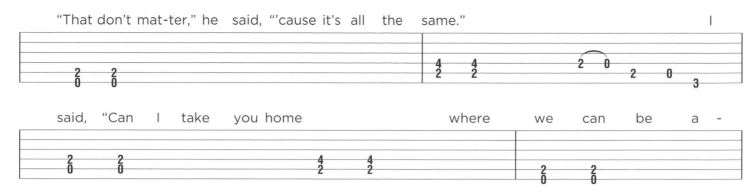

said, "Can I take you home where we can be a -

A5   **N.C.**
lone?" And next we were movin' on; he was with me, yeah, me.

                                   B5
Next, we were movin' on; he was with me, yeah, me, singin',

REPEAT CHORUS 1

VERSE 3

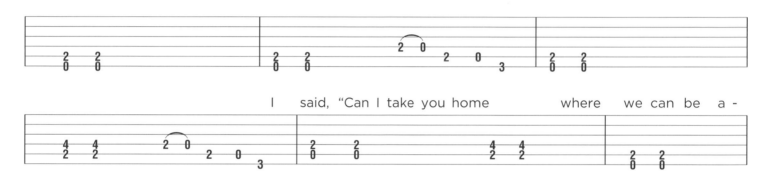

I said, "Can I take you home where we can be a -

A5   **N.C.**
lone?" And next we were movin' on; he was with me, yeah, me.

And we'll be movin' on and singin' that same old song, yeah, with me, singin'

CHORUS 2

N.C.
I love rock 'n' roll, so put another dime in the jukebox, baby.

I love rock 'n' roll, so come, and take your time, and dance with me.

OUTRO-CHORUS

I love rock 'n' roll, so put an-oth-er dime in the juke-box, ba - by.

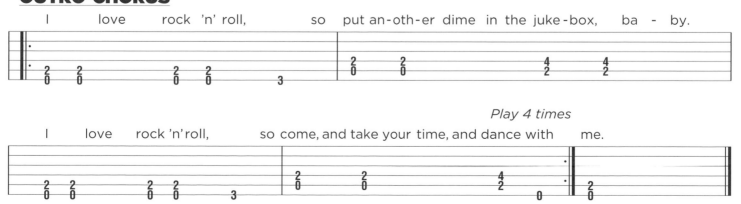

Play 4 times

I love rock 'n' roll, so come, and take your time, and dance with me.

I'm a Believer

featured in the DreamWorks Motion Picture SHREK
Words and Music by Neil Diamond

(Capo 3rd Fret)

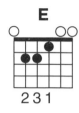 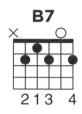  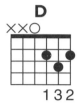

INTRO

Moderately fast

VERSE 1

```
E               B7        E
I thought love was only true in fairy tales,

            B7            E
meant for someone else but not for me.
```

PRE-CHORUS 1

```
A           E       A            E
Love was out to get me.     That's the way it seemed.

A           E          B7          N.C.
   Disappointment haunted all my dreams.
```

CHORUS

```
               E   A   E   A   E    A    E
Then I saw her face;        now I'm a believer.

A   E   A   E   A        E    A    E
Not a trace        of doubt in my mind.

A   E   A   E            D
I'm in love.    I'm a believer. I couldn't leave her if I tried.
```

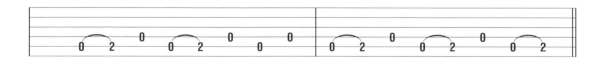

Copyright © 1966 TALLYRAND MUSIC, INC. and EMI FORAY MUSIC
Copyright Renewed
All Rights for TALLYRAND MUSIC, INC. Administered by UNIVERSAL TUNES
All Rights for EMI FORAY MUSIC Administered by SONY/ATV MUSIC PUBLISHING LLC, 424 Church Street, Suite 1200, Nashville, TN 37219
All Rights Reserved   Used by Permission

VERSE 2

E   B7   E
I thought love was more or less a givin' thing.

        B7   E
Seems the more I gave, the less I got.

PRE-CHORUS 2

A   E   A   E
What's the use in tryin'? All you get is pain.

A   E   B7   N.C.
  When I needed sunshine, I got rain.

REPEAT CHORUS

INTERLUDE

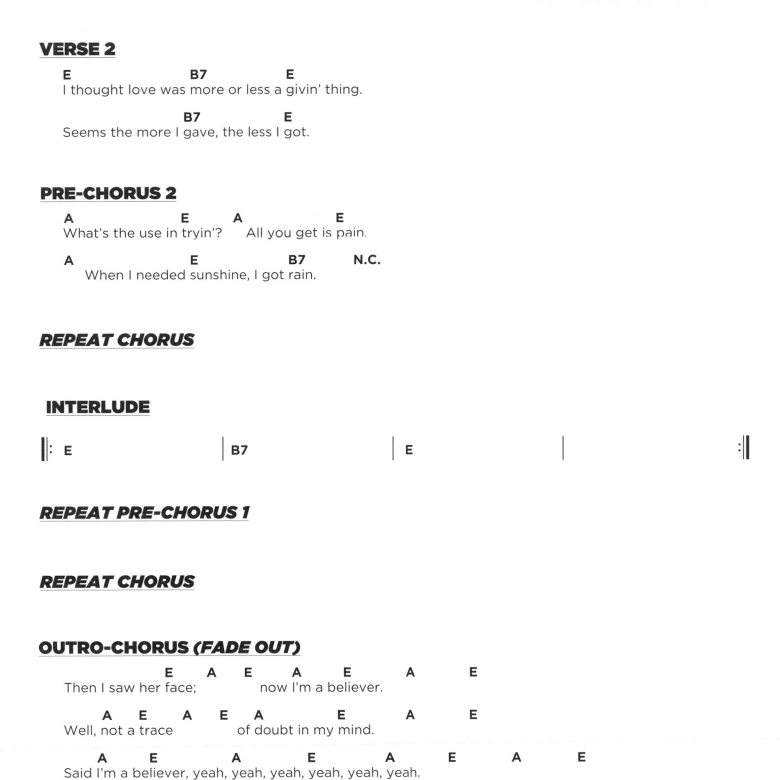

‖: E | B7 | E | :‖

REPEAT PRE-CHORUS 1

REPEAT CHORUS

OUTRO-CHORUS *(FADE OUT)*

      E A E A   E A   E
Then I saw her face;   now I'm a believer.

    A E A E   E   A E
Well, not a trace   of doubt in my mind.

  A   E   A   E   A   E   A   E
Said I'm a believer, yeah, yeah, yeah, yeah, yeah, yeah.

  A E   A E   A E   A E A
Said I'm a believer, yeah.   I said I'm a believer, yeah, yeah, oh.

Let It Go
from FROZEN
Music and Lyrics by Kristen Anderson-Lopez and Robert Lopez

(Capo 1st Fret)

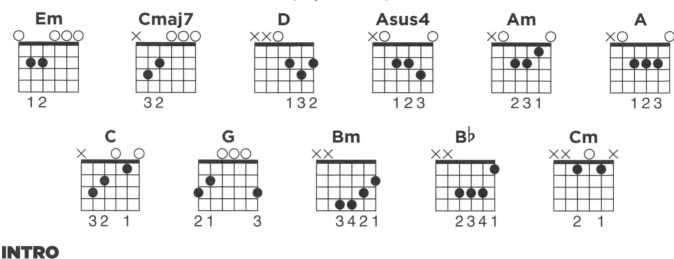

INTRO
Moderately

| Em | Cmaj7 | D | Asus4 Am |

| Em | Cmaj7 | D | Asus4 A |

VERSE 1

Em   Cmaj7   D   Asus4   Am
The snow glows white on the mountain tonight, not a footprint to be seen.

Em   Cmaj7   D   Asus4   A
A kingdom of isolation, and it looks like I'm the queen.

Em   Cmaj7   D   Asus4   Am
The wind is howling like this swirling storm inside.

Em   D   A
Couldn't keep it in, heaven knows I   tried.

PRE-CHORUS 1

D   C
Don't let them in, don't let them see.   Be the good girl you always have to be.

D   C
Conceal, don't feel, don't let them know. Well, now they know.

CHORUS 1

G   D   Em   C   G   D   Em   C
Let it go, let it go. Can't hold it back anymore. Let it go, let it go. Turn away and slam the door.

G   D   Em   C   Bm   Bb
I don't care   what they're going to say.   Let the storm rage on.

C
The cold never bothered me anyway.

Copyright © 2013 Wonderland Music Company, Inc.
All Rights Reserved. Used by Permission.

INTERLUDE

| G | D | ‖ |

VERSE 2

Em   **C**   **D**   **Am**
It's funny how some distance makes everything seem small,

      Em   **D**   **Asus4**   **A**
and the fears that once controlled me can't get to me at all.

PRE-CHORUS 2

D   **C**
It's time to see what I can do   to test the limits and break through.

D   **C**
No right, no wrong, no rules for me. I'm free!

CHORUS 2

     G   **D**   **Em**   **C**   **G**   **D**   **Em**   **C**
Let it go, let it go. I am one with the wind and sky. Let it go, let it go. You'll never see me cry.

G   **D**   **Em**   **C**   **Bm**   **B♭**
Here I stand, and here I'll stay. Let the storm rage on.

BRIDGE

C
My power flurries through the air into the ground. My soul is spiraling in frozen fractals all around.

D
And one thought crystallizes like and icy blast:

Em   **Cmaj7**   **D**   **Am**   **C**
I'm never going back; the past is in the past!

CHORUS 3

     G   **D**   **Em**   **C**   **G**   **D**   **Em**   **C**
Let it go, let it go, and I'll rise like the break of dawn. Let it go, let it go. That perfect girl is gone.

G   **D**   **Em**   **C**   **Cm**   **Bm**   **B♭**
Here I stand in the light of day.   Let the storm rage on.

     C
The cold never bothered me anyway.

Perfect

Words and Music by Ed Sheeran

(Capo 1st fret)

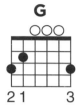  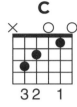 

G	Em	C	D
2 1 3	1 2	3 2 1	1 3 2

VERSE 1

Slow

     G   Em   C   D   G   Em

I found a love for me. Darling, just dive right in, follow my lead. Well, I found a girl, beautiful and sweet.

          C   D   N.C.   G

Well, I never knew you were the someone waiting for me. 'Cause we were just kids when we fell in love,

     Em   C   G D   G   Em

not knowing what it was. I will not give you up this time.   Darling, just kiss me slow, your heart is all

          C   D

I own. And in your eyes, you're holding mine.

CHORUS 1

     Em C   G   D   Em C   G D

Baby, I'm dancing in the dark with you between my arms. Barefoot on the grass, listening to our

Em   C   G   D   Em   C

fav'rite song. When you said you looked a mess, I whispered underneath my breath. But you heard it,

        G   D

darling, you look perfect to -

INTERLUDE

night.

Copyright © 2017 Sony/ATV Music Publishing (UK) Ltd.
All Rights Administered by Sony/ATV Music Publishing LLC, 424 Church Street, Suite 1200, Nashville, TN 37219
International Copyright Secured   All Rights Reserved

VERSE 2

       G   Em   C
Well, I found a woman, stronger than anyone I know. She shares my dreams, I hope that someday,

        D   G   Em   C
I'll share her home. I found a love to carry more than just my secrets, to carry love, to carry children

   D   G   Em   C
of our own. We are still kids, but we're so in love, fighting against all odds. I know we'll be all right

  G D   G   Em   C   D
this time. Darling, just hold my hand. Be my girl, I'll be your man. I've seen the future in your eyes.

CHORUS 2

    Em C   G   D   Em C   G   D
Baby, I'm dancing in the dark with you between my arms.   Barefoot on the grass, listening to our

Em   C   G   D   Em   C
fav'rite song. When I saw you in that dress, looking so beautiful. I don't deserve this, darling,

G   D   G
you look perfect tonight.

CHORUS 3

    Em C   G   D   Em C   G   D
Baby, I'm dancing in the dark with you between my arms. Barefoot in the grass, listening to our

Em   C   G   D   Em C   G   D
fav'rite song. I have faith in what I see, now I know I have met an angel in person and she looks perfect.

  C   D
I don't deserve this; you look perfect to -

OUTRO

night.

Roar

Words and Music by Katy Perry, Max Martin, Dr. Luke,
Bonnie McKee and Henry Walter

(Capo 3rd Fret)

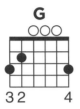

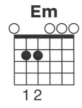
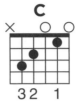
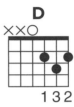

INTRO

Moderately

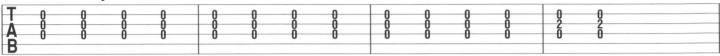

VERSE 1

G
I used to bite my tongue and hold my breath, scared to rock the boat and make a mess. **Am**

Em
So I sat quietly, agreed politely. **C**

G
I guess that I forgot I had a choice. I let you push me past the breaking point. **Am**

Em
I stood for nothing, so I fell for everything. **C**

PRE-CHORUS

G   **Am**
You held me down, but I got up. Already brushing off the dust.

Em   **C**
You hear my voice, you hear that sound like thunder gonna shake the ground.

G   **Am**
You held me down, but I got up. Get ready 'cause I've had enough.

Em   **C**
I see it all, I see it now. I got the eye of the

© 2013 WHEN I'M RICH YOU'LL BE MY BITCH, SONGS OF PULSE RECORDING, PRESCRIPTION SONGS,
BONNIE McKEE MUSIC, WHERE DA KASZ AT?, MXM MUSIC AB, KASZ MONEY PUBLISHING and ONEIROLOGY PUBLISHING
All Rights for WHEN I'M RICH YOU'LL BE MY BITCH Administered by WB MUSIC CORP.
All Rights for PRESCRIPTION SONGS, MXM MUSIC AB, KASZ MONEY PUBLISHING and ONEIROLOGY PUBLISHING
Administered by KOBALT SONGS MUSIC PUBLISHING
All Rights for BONNIE McKEE MUSIC and WHERE DA KASZ AT? Administered by SONGS OF KOBALT PUBLISHING
All Rights Reserved   Used by Permission

CHORUS 1

```
    G                                    Am            Em                                  C
ti - ger, a fighter, dancing through the fi - re 'cause I    am a champion and you're gonna hear    me

       G                    Am            Em                                  C
roar    louder, louder than a li - on, 'cause I    am a champion, and you're gonna hear    me

       G                    Am            Em                              C
roar.    Oh, oh, oh, oh. Oh, oh, oh, oh, oh, oh.    Oh, oh, oh, oh, oh, oh. You're gonna hear    me

       G            N.C.
roar.
```

VERSE 2

```
   G                                           Am
   Now I'm floatin' like a butterfly, stingin' like a bee. I earned my stripes.

   Em                    C
   I went from zero to my own hero.
```

REPEAT PRE-CHORUS

CHORUS 2

```
    G                                    Am            Em                                  C
ti - ger, a fighter, dancing through the fi - re 'cause I    am a champion and you're gonna hear    me

       G                    Am            Em                                  C
roar    louder, louder than a li - on, 'cause I    am a champion, and you're gonna hear    me

       G                    Am            Em                              C
roar.    Oh, oh, oh, oh. Oh, oh, oh, oh, oh, oh.    Oh, oh, oh, oh, oh, oh. You're gonna hear    me

       G                    Am            Em                          C    G
roar.    Oh, oh, oh, oh. Oh, oh, oh, oh, oh, oh.    Oh, oh, oh, oh, oh, oh. You're gonna hear    me roar.
```

INTERLUDE

```
   G              |          Am      |Em                    |
   D                          N.C.
   Roar, oh, roar, oh, roar.    I got the eye of the
```

REPEAT CHORUS 2

Shake It Off

Words and Music by Taylor Swift, Max Martin and Shellback

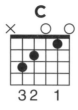
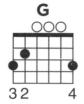

VERSE 1

Fast

Am   C
I stay out too late, got nothing in my brain.

G
That's what people say, mm, mm. That's what people say, mm, mm.

Am   C
I go on too many dates, but I can't make them stay.

G
At least, that's what people say, mm, mm. That's what people say, mm, mm.

PRE-CHORUS

Am   C
But I keep cruisin', can't stop, won't stop movin'. It's like I got this

G
music in my mind sayin', "It's gonna be alright."

CHORUS

Am   C
'Cause the players gonna play, play, play, play, play, and the haters gonna hate, hate, hate, hate, hate.

G
Baby, I'm just gonna shake, shake, shake, shake, shake. I shake it off. I shake it off.

Am   C
Heart-breakers gonna break, break, break, break, break, and the fakers gonna fake, fake, fake, fake, fake.

G
Baby, I'm just gonna shake, shake, shake, shake, shake. I shake it off. I shake it off.

Copyright © 2014 Sony/ATV Music Publishing LLC, Taylor Swift Music and MXM
All Rights on behalf of Sony/ATV Music Publishing LLC and Taylor Swift Music Administered by Sony/ATV Music Publishing LLC,
424 Church Street, Suite 1200, Nashville, TN 37219
All Rights on behalf of MXM Administered Worldwide by Kobalt Songs Music Publishing
International Copyright Secured   All Rights Reserved

VERSE 2

         Am   C

I never miss a beat. I'm lightning on my feet,

                     G

and that's what they don't see, mm, mm. That's what they don't see, mm, mm.

         Am   C

I'm dancin' on my own. I make the moves up as I go,

                     G

and that's what they don't know, mm, mm. That's what they don't know, mm, mm.

PRE-CHORUS 2

         Am   C

But I keep cruisin', can't stop, won't stop groovin'. It's like I got this

G   N.C.

music in my mind sayin', "It's gonna be alright."

REPEAT CHORUS

BRIDGE

    Am   C

I shake it off. I shake it off. I, I, I shake it off. I shake it off. I, I,

  G

I shake it off. I shake it off. I, I, I shake it off. I shake it off.

BREAKDOWN

N.C.

    Hey, hey, hey. Just think while you've been gettin' down and out about the liars and the dirty, dirty

cheats of the world, you coulda been gettin' down to this sick beat.

My ex-man brought his new girlfriend. She's like, "Oh my God!" But I'm just gonna shake. And to the

fella over there with the hella good hair, won't you come on over, baby? We can shake, shake, shake.

REPEAT CHORUS

REPEAT BRIDGE (2 TIMES)

A Sky Full of Stars

Words and Music by Guy Berryman, Jon Buckland, Will Champion,
Chris Martin and Tim Bergling

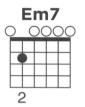 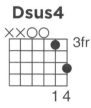 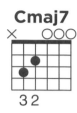 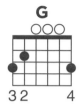 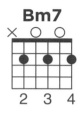 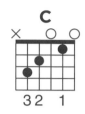 

INTRO

Moderately

‖: Em7   Dsus4 | Cmaj7 | G | Bm7   :‖

VERSE 1

Em7 Dsus4   Cmaj7   G   Bm7
'Cause you're a sky, 'cause you're a sky full of stars.

Em7 Dsus4 Cmaj7   G   Bm7
I'm gonna give you my heart.

Em7 Dsus4   Cmaj7   G   Bm7
'Cause you're a sky, 'cause you're a sky full of stars.

Em7 Dsus4   Cmaj7   G   Bm7
'Cause you light up the path.

CHORUS 1

Em7 Dsus4 C   G   Bm7
I don't   care. Go on and tear me apart.

Em7 Dsus4 C   G   Bm7
I don't   care if you do, ooh, ooh, ooh.

Em7 Dsus4   Cmaj7   G   Bm7
'Cause in a sky, 'cause in a sky full of stars, I think I saw

Em7 Dsus4   C   G   Bm7
you.

REPEAT INTRO (3 TIMES)

Copyright © 2014 by Universal Music Publishing MGB Ltd. and EMI Blackwood Music Inc.
All Rights for Universal Music Publishing MGB Ltd. in the United States and Canada Administered by Universal Music - MGB Songs
All Rights for EMI Blackwood Music Inc. Administered by Sony/ATV Publishing LLC, 424 Church Street, Suite 1200, Nashville, TN 37219
International Copyright Secured   All Rights Reserved

VERSE 2

Em7 Dsus4   **Cmaj7**   **G**   **Bm7**
'Cause you're a sky, 'cause you're a sky full of stars.

Em7 Dsus4 Cmaj7 G   **Bm7**
I wanna   die in your arms.

Em7 Dsus4   **Cmaj7 G**   **Bm7**
'Cause you get lighter the more it gets dark.

Em7 Dsus4   **Cmaj7**   **G**   **Bm7**
I'm gonna give you my heart.

CHORUS 2

Em7   **Dsus4 C**   **G**   **Bm7**
But I don't   care. Go on and tear me apart.

Em7   **Dsus4 C**   **G**   **Bm7**
But I don't   care if you do, ooh, ooh, ooh.

Em7 Dsus4   **Cmaj7**   **G**   **Bm7**
'Cause in a sky, 'cause in a sky full of stars, I think I see

Em7 Dsus4   **C**   **G**   **Bm7**
you.   I think I see

Em7 Dsus4   **C**   **G**   **N.C.**
you.

REPEAT INTRO (4 TIMES)

OUTRO

C	**D**	**Em7**		**G**

C   **D**   **Em7**   **G**
'Cause you're a sky, you're a sky full of stars, such a heavenly

C   **D**   **Em7**   **G**
view.   You're such a heavenly

C   **D**   **Em7**   **G**
view.

Play 3 times

C	**D**	**Em7**			**N.C.**

Story of My Life

Words and Music by Jamie Scott, John Henry Ryan, Julian Bunetta, Harry Styles,
Liam Payne, Louis Tomlinson, Niall Horan and Zain Malik

(Capo 3rd Fret)

 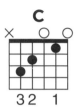 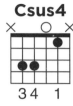 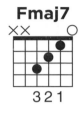  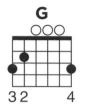 

Am	C	Csus4	Fmaj7	F	G	Dm7
2 3 1	3 2 1	3 4 1	3 2 1	3 2 1 1	3 2 4	2 1 1

INTRO

Moderately

‖: Am | | | C   Csus4 | C :‖

VERSE 1

Am   C   Csus4   C
Written in these walls are the stories that I can't explain.

Am   C   Csus4   C
I leave my heart open, but it stays right here empty for days.

Am   Fmaj7   C   Csus4   C
She told me in the mornin' she don't feel the same about us in her bones.

Am   Fmaj7   C   Csus4   C
Seems to me that when I die, these words will be written on my stone.

PRE-CHORUS 1

        F   G   Am   F   G   Am
And I'll be gone, gone tonight. The ground beneath my feet is open wide.

        F   G   Am   G
The way that I've been holdin' on too tight with nothin' in between.

CHORUS 1

C   F   Am   F   C
The story of my life. I take her home. I drive all night to keep her warm, and time is fro - zen.

                            F   Am   F   C
The story of my life. I give her hope. I spend her love until she's broke inside.   The story of my life.

Copyright © 2013 EMI Music Publishing Ltd., BMG Platinum Songs, Music Of Big Deal, The Family Songbook, Bob Erotik Music,
Holy Cannoli Music and PPM Music Ltd.
All Rights on behalf of EMI Publishing Ltd. Administered by Sony/ATV Music Publishing LLC, 424 Church Street, Suite 1200, Nashville, TN 37219
All Rights on behalf of BMG Platinum Songs, Music Of Big Deal, The Family Songbook and Bob Erotik Music
Administered by BMG Rights Management (US) LLC
All Rights on behalf of Holy Cannoli Music Administered by Songs of Universal, Inc.
All Rights on behalf of PPM Music Ltd. Administered by Downtown DLJ Songs
International Copyright Secured   All Rights Reserved

VERSE 2

Am   C   Csus4   C
Written on these walls are the colors that I can't change.

Am   C   Csus4   C
Leave my heart open, but it stays right here in its cage.

Am   Fmaj7   C   Csus4   C
I know that in the mornin' now, I see a single light upon the hill.

Am   Fmaj7   C   Csus4   C
Although I am broken, my heart is untamed still.

PRE-CHORUS 2

F   G   Am   F   G   Am
And I'll be gone, gone tonight. The fire beneath my feet is burnin' bright.

F   G   Am   G
The way that I've been holdin' on so tight with nothin' in between.

REPEAT CHORUS 1

BRIDGE

Dm7   G   Dm7   G
And I'll be waitin' for this time to come around, but baby, runnin' after you is like chasin' the clouds.

CHORUS 2

C   F   Am   Fmaj7
The story of my life. I take her home. I drive all night to keep her warm, and time is frozen.

C   F   Am   F   C
The story of my life. I give her hope. I spend her love until she's broke inside.   The story of my life.

OUTRO

C   F   Am   F
The story of my life.   The story of my life.

C
The story of my life.

Superheroes

Words and Music by Danny O'Donoghue, Mark Sheehan and James Barry

(Capo 1st Fret)

 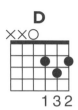  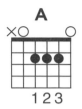 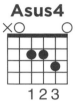  

INTRO

Moderately slow

| G | D | | Bm7 | A | | G | D | | Asus4 | A | |

| G | D | | Bm7 | A | | G | D | | A | |

VERSE 1

G   D   Bm7   A
All her life, she has seen all the meaner side of mean.

        G   D   Asus4   A
They took away the prophet's dream for a profit on the street.

        D   G   A   N.C.
Now she's stronger than you know. A heart of steel starts to grow.

VERSE 2

        G   D   Bm7   A
All his life, he's been told he'll be nothin' when he's old.

        G   D   Bm7   A
All the kicks and all the blows, he won't ever let it show.

        D   G   A   N.C.
'Cause he's stronger than you know, a heart of steel starts to grow.

CHORUS

            G   D   Bm7   A
When you've been fightin' for it all your life, you've been strugglin' to make things right,

            G   D   A
that's how a superhero learns to fly.

            G   D   Bm7 A
When you've been fightin' for it all your life, you've been workin' every day and night,

            G   D   A
that's how a superhero learns to fly.

INTERLUDE 1

| G | D | | Bm7 | A | |

Copyright © 2013, 2014 Global Talent Publishing Ltd. and Madnotes Production Ltd.
All Rights for Global Talent Publishing Ltd. in the U.S. and Canada Administered by Songs of Global Entertainment
All Rights for Madnotes Production Ltd. Administered Worldwide by Kobalt Songs Music Publishing
All Rights Reserved   Used by Permission

VERSE 3

```
         G        D         Bm7        A
All the hurt, all the lies, all the tears that they cry.

         G             D         Bm7      A
When the moment is just right, you see fire in their eyes.

         D         G             A              N.C.
'Cause he's stronger than you know, a heart of steel starts to grow.
```

REPEAT CHORUS

INTERLUDE 2

```
‖: G     D              | Bm7    A          | G     D          | A          :‖
```

BRIDGE

```
         G                D                      Bm7          A
She's got lions in her heart,     a fire in her soul. He's got a beast in his belly that's so hard to control.

         G             D
'Cause they've taken too much hits, take 'em blow by blow.

     Asus4              A
Now light a match, stand back, watch 'em explode.

     Em7        Gmaj7                   D          A
She's got lions in her heart,        a fire in her soul. He's got a beast in his belly that's so hard to control.

         D             G
'Cause they've taken too much hits, take 'em blow by blow.

     Asus4                          A                  N.C.
Now light a match, stand back, watch 'em explode, explode, explode, explode, explode.
```

REPEAT CHORUS

REPEAT INTERLUDE 2 (2 TIMES)

OUTRO-CHORUS

```
                    G    D                        Bm7      A
When you've been fightin' for it all your life, you've been strugglin' to make things right,

                    G    D         A
that's how a superhero learns to fly.
```

We Got the Beat

Words and Music by Charlotte Caffey

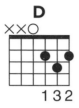 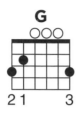 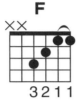 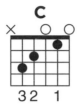 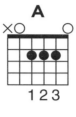 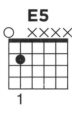

INTRO

Play 4 times

Moderately

VERSE 1

w/ Intro Riff
See the people walkin' down the street, fall in line just watchin' all their feet.

They don't know where they want to go, but they're

walk - in'   in   time.

CHORUS 1

           D   G   F   C
They got the beat, they got the beat, they got the beat. Yeah, they got the beat.

REPEAT INTRO (2 TIMES)

VERSE 2

w/ Intro Riff
All the kids just gettin' out of school, they can't wait to hang out and be cool.

Hang around till quarter-after twelve, that's

when they   fall   in   line.

Copyright © 1981 by Universal Music - MGB Songs
International Copyright Secured   All Rights Reserved

CHORUS 2

               D   **G**   **F**   **C**

They got the beat, they got the beat, kids got the beat. Yeah, kids got the beat.

REPEAT INTRO (2 TIMES)

VERSE 3

w/ Intro Riff
Go-go music really makes us dance. Do The Pony, puts us in a trance.

Do Watusi, just give us a chance, that's

when they   fall   in   line.

```
|------------------------------------------------|------------------------------------------------||
|------------------------------------------------|------------------------------------------------||
|--2----2----2----2----2----2----2----2---|--2----2----2----2----2----2----2----2---||
|--0----0----0----0----0----0----0----0---|--0----0----0----0----0----0----0----0---||
|------------------------------------------------|------------------------------------------------||
|------------------------------------------------|------------------------------------------------||
```

CHORUS 3

               D   **G**   **F**   **C**

'Cause we got the beat, we got the beat, we got the beat. Yeah, we got it!

INTERLUDE

A   **N.C.**

        We got the beat. We got the beat. We got the beat.

Everybody get on your feet. We know you can dance to the beat.

                            E5

Jump back, get down. Round and round and round.

OUTRO

w/ Intro Riff
We got the beat. We got the beat. We got the beat.

We got the beat. We got the beat. We got the beat.

          We   got   the   beat.

```
|---------------------------------------------------|-------------------||
|---------------------------------------------------|-------------------||
|--2----2----------------------------------------|-------------------||
|--0----0----0----0----0----0----0----0---|--0---------------||
|---------------------------------------------------|-------------------||
|---------------------------------------------------|-------------------||
```

What About Us

Words and Music by Alecia Moore, Steve Mac and Johnny McDaid

(Capo 1st Fret)

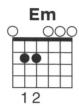 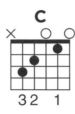 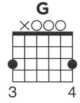 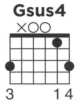

INTRO

Moderately

| Em | | C | | G   Gsus4   G | | Gsus4   G | |

| Em | C | G   Gsus4   G | Gsus4 |

La, da, da, da, da. La, da, da, da, da.   Da, da, da,   da.

VERSE 1

G   Em   C   G   Gsus4   G   Gsus4

We are search-lights, we can see in the dark.

G   Em   C   G   Gsus4   G   Gsus4

We are rock - ets pointed up at the stars.

G   Em   C   G   Gsus4   G   Gsus4

We are bil - lions of beautiful hearts.

G   Em   C   G   Gsus4   G   Gsus4

And you sold   us down the river too far.

CHORUS

G   Em   C   G   Gsus4   G   Gsus4

What about us? What about all the times you said you had the answers?

G   Em   C   G   Gsus4   G   Gsus4

What about us? What about all the broken, happy ever-afters?

G   Em   C   G   Gsus4   G   Gsus4

What about us? What about all the plans that ended in disaster?

G   Em   C   G   Gsus4   G   Gsus4

What about love? What about trust? What about   us?

Copyright © 2017 EMI Blackwood Music Inc., Pink Inside Publishing, Rokstone Music and Spirit B-Unique JV S.à.r.l.
All Rights on behalf of EMI Blackwood Music Inc. and Pink Inside Publishing Administered by Sony/ATV Music Publishing LLC,
424 Church Street, Suite 1200, Nashville, TN 37219
All Rights on behalf of Rokstone Music in the United States and Canada Administered by Universal - PolyGram International Publishing, Inc.
All Rights on behalf of Spirit B-Unique JV S.à.r.l. in the U.S. and Canada Administered by Spirit One Music and
Worldwide excluding the U.S. and Canada by Kobalt Music Ltd.
International Copyright Secured   All Rights Reserved

VERSE 2

```
G       Em     C                      G      Gsus4    G         Gsus4
We are prob  -  lems that want to be solved.

G       Em     C                      G    Gsus4    G       Gsus4
We are chil  -  dren that need to be loved.

G         Em    C                     G      Gsus4    G          Gsus4
We were will  -  in', we came when you called.

          G       Em    C             G     Gsus4    G         Gsus4
But man, you fooled us; enough is enough.
```

REPEAT CHORUS

INTERLUDE

```
‖: Em                |  C                   |  G     Gsus4    G    |       Gsus4     G  :‖

          Em           C                    G    Gsus4    G         Gsus4
What about us? What about all the plans that ended in disaster?

G       Em            C                 G      Gsus4    G       Gsus4    G
What about love? What about trust? What about     us?
```

BRIDGE

```
Em                       C                     G     Gsus4  G       Gsus4  G
Sticks and stones, they may break these bones, but then     I'll be read  -  y. Are you read  -  y?

Em           C                  G       Gsus4  G       Gsus4  G
It's the start of us waking up, come on.     Are you read  -  y? I'll be read  -  y.

Em              C               G       Gsus4  G       Gsus4  G
I don't want control. I want to let go.     Are you read  -  y? I'll be read  -  y.

          Em          C         G       Gsus4  G    N.C.
'Cause now it's time to let them know.     We are read  -  y.     What about...
```

REPEAT CHORUS

OUTRO

```
          G    Em           C          G    Gsus4      G          Gsus4
What about us? What about us? What about     us?

          G    Em           C          N.C.
What about us? What about us? What about     us?
```

Whatever It Takes

Words and Music by Dan Reynolds, Wayne Sermon, Ben McKee,
Daniel Platzman and Joel Little

(Capo 1st Fret)

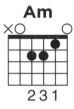 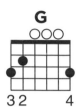 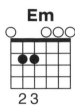 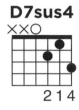 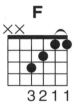 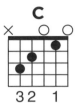

INTRO

Moderately fast

‖: Am | G | Em | :‖

VERSE 1

Am   **G**
Fallin' too fast to prepare for this, trippin' in the world could be dangerous.

Em
Everybody circlin', it's vulturous, negative, nepotist.

Am   **G**
Everybody waitin' for the fall of man, everybody prayin' for the end of times.

Em
Everybody hopin' they could be the one. I was born to run, I was born for this.

PRE-CHORUS

Am   **G**   **D7sus4**   **Em**
Whip, whip, run me like a race horse. Pull me like a ripcord. Break me down, and build me up.

                    Am   **G**   **D7sus4**
I want to be the slip, slip, word upon your lip, lip. Letter that you rip, rip.

               Em
Break me down, and build me up.

CHORUS

               F   **C**   **G**   **Am**
Whatever it takes   'cause I love the adrenaline in my veins.

               F   **C**   **G**   **Am**
I do whatever it takes   'cause I love how it feels when I break the chains.

               F   **C**   **G**   **Am**
Whatever it takes,   you take me to the top. I'm ready for

          F   **C**   **G**   **Am**   N.C.
whatever it takes   'cause I love the adrenaline in my veins.   I do what it takes.

Copyright © 2017 SONGS OF UNIVERSAL, INC., SONGS FOR KIDINAKORNER,
IMAGINE DRAGONS PUBLISHING and EMI BLACKWOOD MUSIC INC.
All Rights for SONGS FOR KIDINAKORNER and IMAGINE DRAGONS PUBLISHING Administered by SONGS OF UNIVERSAL, INC.
All Rights for EMI BLACKWOOD MUSIC INC. Administered by SONY/ATV MUSIC PUBLISHING LLC,
424 Church Street, Suite 1200, Nashville, TN 37219
All Rights Reserved   Used by Permission

VERSE 2

Am   **G**
Always had a fear of bein' typical, lookin' at my body, feelin' miserable.

Em
Always hangin' on to the visual. I want to be invisible.

Am   **G**
Lookin' at my years like a martyrdom, everybody needs to be a part of 'em.

Em
Never be enough, I'm the prodigal son. I was born to run. I was born for this.

REPEAT PRE-CHORUS

REPEAT CHORUS

BRIDGE

Am   **G**
Hypocritical, egotistical, don't want to be the

Em
parenthetical, hypothetical. Workin' onto

Am   **G**
somethin' that I'm proud of, out of the box, an

  Em
epoxy to the world and the vision we've lost. I'm an

  Am   **G**
apostrophe. I'm just a symbol to remind you that there's

Em
more to see. I'm just a product of the system, a

  Am   **G**
catastrophe. And yet a masterpiece, and yet I'm

Em
half-diseased. And when I am deceased, at least I

Am   **G**
go down to the grave and die happily. Leave the

Em
body of my soul to be a part of me.

N.C.
        I do what it takes.

REPEAT CHORUS

Guitar Chord Songbooks

Each 6" x 9" book includes complete lyrics, chord symbols, and guitar chord diagrams.

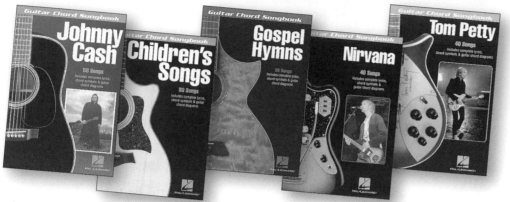

Acoustic Hits 00701787 . . . . $14.99	**The Doors** 00699888 . . . . $19.99	**Steve Miller** 00701146 . . . . $12.99
Acoustic Rock 00699540 . . . . $22.99	**Eagles** 00122917 . . . . $17.99	**Modern Worship** 00701801 . . . . $16.99
Alabama 00699914 . . . . $14.95	**Early Rock** 00699916 . . . . $14.99	**Motown** 00699734 . . . . $19.99
The Beach Boys 00699566 . . . . $19.99	**Folksongs** 00699541 . . . . $14.99	**Willie Nelson** 00148273 . . . . $17.99
Bluegrass 00702585 . . . . $14.99	**Folk Pop Rock** 00699651 . . . . $17.99	**Nirvana** 00699762 . . . . $17.99
Johnny Cash 00699648 . . . . $19.99	**40 Easy Strumming Songs** 00115972 . . . . $16.99	**Roy Orbison** 00699752 . . . . $19.99
Children's Songs 00699539 . . . . $17.99	**Four Chord Songs** 00701611 . . . . $15.99	**Peter, Paul & Mary** 00103013 . . . . $19.99
Christmas Carols 00699536 . . . . $14.99	**Glee** 00702501 . . . . $14.99	**Tom Petty** 00699883 . . . . $17.99
Christmas Songs 00119911 . . . . $14.99	**Gospel Hymns** 00700463 . . . . $16.99	**Pink Floyd** 00139116 . . . . $17.99
Eric Clapton 00699567 . . . . $19.99	**Grand Ole Opry®** 00699885 . . . . $16.95	**Pop/Rock** 00699538 . . . . $16.99
Classic Rock 00699598 . . . . $20.99	**Grateful Dead** 00139461 . . . . $16.99	**Praise & Worship** 00699634 . . . . $14.99
Coffeehouse Hits 00703318 . . . . $14.99	**Green Day** 00103074 . . . . $16.99	**Elvis Presley** 00699633 . . . . $17.99
Country 00699534 . . . . $17.99	**Irish Songs** 00701044 . . . . $16.99	**Queen** 00702395 . . . . $14.99
Country Favorites 00700609 . . . . $14.99	**Michael Jackson** 00137847 . . . . $14.99	**Red Hot Chili Peppers** 00699710 . . . . $24.99
Country Hits 00140859 . . . . $14.99	**Billy Joel** 00699632 . . . . $19.99	**The Rolling Stones** 00137716 . . . . $19.99
Country Standards 00700608 . . . . $12.95	**Elton John** 00699732 . . . . $17.99	**Bob Seger** 00701147 . . . . $12.99
Cowboy Songs 00699636 . . . . $19.99	**Ray LaMontagne** 00130337 . . . . $12.99	**Carly Simon** 00121011 . . . . $14.99
Creedence Clearwater Revival 00701786 . . . . $16.99	**Latin Songs** 00700973 . . . . $14.99	**Sting** 00699921 . . . . $24.99
Jim Croce 00148087 . . . . $14.99	**Love Songs** 00701043 . . . . $14.99	**Three Chord Acoustic Songs** 00123860 . . . . $14.99
Crosby, Stills & Nash 00701609 . . . . $16.99	**Bob Marley** 00701704 . . . . $17.99	**Three Chord Songs** 00699720 . . . . $17.99
John Denver 02501697 . . . . $17.99	**Bruno Mars** 00125332 . . . . $12.99	**Two-Chord Songs** 00119236 . . . . $16.99
Neil Diamond 00700606 . . . . $19.99	**Paul McCartney** 00385035 . . . . $16.95	**U2** 00137744 . . . . $19.99
Disney – 2nd Edition 00295786 . . . . $17.99		**Hank Williams** 00700607 . . . . $16.99
		Stevie Wonder 00120862 . . . . $14.99

Prices and availability subject to change without notice.

Visit Hal Leonard online at **www.halleonard.com**

1221
480